I0201870

A 31-Day Journey to
Rise Toward Victory and
Success Every Day

BELIEVE
you can reign in life

Evangeline Colbert

BELIEVE YOU CAN REIGN IN LIFE!

Unless otherwise indicated, Scripture quotations are taken from the Holy Bible King James Version or from the New King James Version®. Copyright © 1982 by Thomas Nelson, Inc. Used by permission. All rights reserved. Scripture quotations marked (NLT) are taken from the Holy Bible, New Living Translation, copyright © 1996, 2004, 2007 by Tyndale House Foundation. Used by permission of Tyndale House Publishers, Inc., Carol Stream, Illinois 60188. All rights reserved.
Scripture quotations marked (NIV) THE HOLY BIBLE, NEW INTERNATIONAL VERSION®, NIV® Copyright © 1973, 1978, 1984, 2011 by Biblica, Inc.TM Used by permission. All rights reserved worldwide. Scripture quotations marked (MSG) are taken from *The Message*. Copyright 1993, 1994, 1995, 1996, 2000, 2001, 2002. Used by permission of NavPress Publishing Group.
Scripture quotations marked (AMP) are taken from the Amplified® Bible, Copyright © 1954, 1958, 1962, 1964, 1965, 1987 by   The Lockman Foundation. Used by permission. (www.Lockman.org)
Scripture quotations marked "TLB" or "The Living Bible" are taken from The Living Bible [computer file] / Kenneth N. Taylor.—electronic ed.— Wheaton : Tyndale House, 1997, c1971 by Tyndale House Publishers, Inc. Used by permission. All rights reserved.
Scripture quotations marked "GW" are taken from GOD'S WORD®, © 1995 God's Word to the Nations. Used by permission of Baker Publishing Group.
Scripture quotations marked TPT are from The Passion Translation®. Copyright © 2017, 2018 by Passion & Fire Ministries, Inc. Used by permission. All rights reserved. ThePassionTranslation.com.

BELIEVE - A 31-Day Devotional
Copyright © 2020 by Evangeline Colbert
Published by iHope Publishing
ISBN: 978-0-9858303-8-0

Cover Design by Joy McMillan at SimplyBloom.org

All rights reserved. No part of this publication may be reproduced, stored in a retrieval system, or transmitted in any form or by any means---electronic, mechanical, digital, photocopy, recording, or any other—except for brief quotations in printed reviews, without the prior permission of the author or publisher.

A DARE

I dare you to spend time over the next 31 days on a journey with me that will lift you to higher heights!

You'll see a difference as you saturate yourself in the transformational words about the victory that Jesus *already* won for you. Will you set aside 7-10 minutes at the start of each day to renew and redirect your mind so that throughout the day you are expecting good things to happen to you?

Will you commit to focus on God's love for *you*? He created you to live as a winner. Make a decision right now to immerse yourself in a daily reading and then look for ways to incorporate God's promises into your daily life so that you **live to win**!

Do this for YOU! 🖤

Evangeline

P.S. Remember, life changes when we change what we believe!

BELIEVE YOU CAN REIGN IN LIFE!

WITH GOD, YOU CAN STOP LIVING LIKE A VICTIM... YOU WERE CREATED TO BE A VICTOR!

-Quote from "Live to Win" book

Day 1

Sit in a Place of Honor

Victory Verse

Rise from the dust. Sit in a place of honor. -Isaiah 52:2 NLT

Winner's Inspiration

It's hard to step aside and let someone else take on what we see as *our* work or *our* battle. But instead of working up a sweat to force good things to happen in your life, God wants you to rest in Him and allow Him to do the heavy lifting. He wants you to rise from your dusty place of self-effort and sit in a place of honor where you enjoy His favor in every aspect of your life. He wants you **seated in the position of honor** that Jesus' sacrifice on the cross made possible for you.

God wants you to rest while He does the work of battle against the enemy of your success. Allow God's grace—His unearned, unmerited, and "sweatless" favor—to work on your behalf. Let the ultimate Victor show you *how to stop being a victim of your circumstances*. He wants to show you how to let go, enjoy His flow, and **live to win**.

Winner's Viewpoint

You won't be defeated when you're seated (see Ephesians 2:6).

Victory Prayer Starter

Lord Jesus, I want to sit in the place of honor Your death provided for me. Please help me let You do the heavy lifting in my circumstances of

_____

_____

_____

_____

_____

Today, I'm grateful for this Win:

Thank you, Lord Jesus, for how You gave me victory in

_____

_____

_____

_____

_____

Day 2

Victories Don't Come by Accident

Victory Verse

"I am the vine; you are the branches. If you remain in Me and I in you, you will bear much fruit; apart from Me you can do nothing.
John 15:5

Winner's Inspiration

You need a strategy if you want to win in life. And that strategy must include Jesus because He said that you can do nothing without Him. Your success in every aspect of life and your ability to live "the abundant life" are wrapped up in Him.

What should you incorporate into your daily routine so you can experience more victories? God is *for* you and not against you. He loves you and wants you to **live to win**! He loves you with a "no matter what" kind of love. No matter what you've done or haven't done, He will always love you. And because He loves you, He only wants the best for you. His desire is to give you anything and everything that is good so that you can enjoy life.

But the enemy of your success would like nothing better than to distract and deceive you, making you think that you don't matter to God. You *do* matter to Him. Rest assured, God hears you, He sees you, and He cares about what you experience in life.

Winner's Viewpoint

Good success is in God's playbook for you.
Use His strategy for your victory.

Victory Prayer Starter

Lord Jesus, help me to focus on You and not my problems of

_____

_____

_____

Today, I'm grateful for this Win:

Thank you, Lord Jesus, for how You gave me victory in

_____

_____

_____

_____

Day 3

Quality of Life - Here and Now

Victory Verse

For if you tell others with your own mouth that Jesus Christ is your Lord and believe in your own heart that God has raised him from the dead, you will be saved.
Romans 10:9 TLB

Winner's Inspiration

God has a system and everything works according to His system, whether or not we choose to adhere to it *and* whether we choose to believe it or not. Just like the law of gravity works for everyone whether they believe it or not, God's love for every human being exists, whether they believe He loves them or not.

Scripture shows us that God wants only the best in life for us. That desire is based upon His everlasting and unfailing love for us. Can you believe that He loves *you* and that He is a loving Rewarder, not an unrelenting Punisher? He wants to save us, keep us safe and sound, and to remain ever on-point to rescue us from danger and destruction while we live here on earth. That destruction does not only exist in the place of Hell after death; it exists during life on earth in the form of injury, poverty, dysfunctional relationships, suffering, and more.

God sent Jesus so that He could rescue us from *all* of that. Because of His great love for us, He prefers to see us delivered, favored, prospering, healed to wholeness, and restored.

Winner's Viewpoint

Salvation is not only about going to heaven after death; it's about the quality of life you live here on earth.

Victory Prayer Starter

Lord Jesus, in this present moment, I trust You to:

_____

_____

_____

_____

Today, I'm grateful for this Win:

Thank you, Lord Jesus, for how You gave me victory in

_____

_____

_____

Day 4

Hit a Home Run in Life

Victory Verse

*But now, how much more are we held in the grip of grace and
continue reigning as kings in life, enjoying our regal freedom
through the gift of perfect righteousness
in the one and only Jesus, the Messiah!*
Romans 5:17 TPT

Winner's Inspiration

Jesus desires for us to be victors and to reign in this life on earth, not to have to wait until we get to heaven. He wants us to hit a home run in life.

Here's an illustration: When you play the game of baseball, you must have the right equipment and training when you step up to the plate. If you want to have a chance of hitting a home run, you have to have a bat to hit the ball. Stepping up to the plate with a roll of wrapping paper instead of a bat will not make that ball go very far.

Similarly, playing the game of life in God's ballpark, you have to use the right equipment as well, and follow his principles in order to hit that home run in life. The equipment we use in God's ballpark is His Word, found in the Bible and the training is practicing consistent prayer. When we use His Word, we are putting Him first, and we open ourselves to experience more of how He wants us to rest in Christ.

Winner's Viewpoint

Living your best life is possible when you believe God's Word and incorporate it into your day.

Victory Prayer Starter

Lord Jesus, show me how to use your Word in my life in order to

_____

_____

_____

Today, I'm grateful for this Win:

Thank you, Lord Jesus, for how You gave me victory in

_____

_____

_____

_____

_____

Day 5

Taking the Elevator

Victory Verse

Rest in the Lord and wait patiently for Him. Psalm 37:7

Winner's Inspiration

Belief is having confidence in the truth or reliability of something without having absolute tangible proof. It means having a conviction that Jesus is able *and* willing to come to your rescue, that He is on your side.

You can **live to win** by climbing the proverbial ladder of success through your own effort or you can do so by resting—believing in the finished work that Jesus did on your behalf on the cross. It's the difference between taking the stairs to the top of a skyscraper and taking the elevator. Either way, you reach the top but getting there is much easier, less tiring, and faster via the elevator. When you choose to **live to win** by believing Jesus is your source of all things good, it's like taking a *spiritual* elevator.

BELIEVE YOU CAN REIGN IN LIFE!

Winner's Viewpoint

Take comfort in knowing that Jesus has opened the elevator

door for you to rise to success.

Victory Prayer Starter

Lord Jesus, I want my victory and success to reflect

_____

_____

_____

_____

Today, I'm grateful for this Win:

Thank you, Lord Jesus, for how You gave me victory in

_____

_____

_____

_____

_____

Day 6

An Intimate Relationship

Victory Verse

*We have known and believed that God loves us. God is love.
Those who live in God's love live in God,
and God lives in them.–* 1 John 4:16 GW

Winner's Inspiration

Believe that God loves you. That's first and foremost. God's nature is to always love. God *is* love and He wants you to believe His love is continually being poured out to you (1 John 4:8,16). Develop an intimate relationship with Him as you focus on His love for you and the unearned favor that He abundantly pours out.

Do you ever question the sincerity of Jesus, His attention to details, and even His love? Regardless of the doubts and delays you might experience, Jesus wants you to trust Him — to fear not, to only believe.

When you believe His love, you have confidence and boldness and there's no room for fear to overwhelm you! Keep believing

God's Word. No matter what, keep believing in God's love for YOU.

Believe that through His finished work on the cross, Jesus has already put you in a position of victory. You don't have to wait until you get to heaven; the victory is *already* yours.

Winner's Viewpoint

Believe that God loves YOU, just as you are.

Victory Prayer Starter

Lord Jesus, because You said that I am in You and You are in me, I believe that

_____

_____

_____

_____

Today, I'm grateful for this Win:

Thank you, Lord Jesus, for how You gave me victory in

_____

_____

_____

_____

_____

Day 7

Is it God's Fault?

Victory Verse

The thief comes only in order to steal and kill and destroy.
I came that they may have and enjoy life, and have it in
abundance (to the full, till it overflows).
John 10:10 AMP

Winner's Inspiration

Have you ever believed that God is the cause for your negative circumstances? The devil is actually the one that causes all the interjection of tragedy into your life. God wants you to experience only joy, peace, and goodness. When you believe God is the source of tragedy instead of your source of triumph, you are believing wrong.

So many times, especially during the trials of life, people blame God for their misfortunes and troubles. They tend to think that He is punishing them for something they did wrong.

But we are clearly shown in John 10:10 that it is the devil that comes into our circumstance to *kill* our dreams, *steal* our joy, and *destroy* our hope of anything good coming our way. Keep reading to the end of that verse and be encouraged by it—Jesus came to bring us life. He brings life to our dreams, life to our relationships, life to our finances, and life to our bodies and minds. He presents us with such an abundance of life that it overflows from us to others, enabling us to reach out and help others **live to win**.

Winner's Viewpoint

Jesus came to bring only victory and goodness into your life.

Victory Prayer Starter

Lord Jesus, when I have doubts about Your goodness, please

_____

_____

_____

_____

Today, I'm grateful for this Win:

Thank you, Lord Jesus, for how You gave me victory in

_____

_____

_____

Day 8

The Thread

Victory Verse

*Death and life are in the power of the tongue, and those who
love it and indulge it will eat its fruit and
bear the consequences of their words.*
Proverbs 18:21 AMP

Winner's Inspiration

Your thought-life greatly influences how you experience life. Your repeated thoughts will inevitably give rise to words that align with them. Did you know that your words have the power to bring positive energy (life) or negative energy (death) to your circumstances (Proverbs 18:21)? As you hear yourself say these words more and more, they influence the decisions you make and the actions you take. Your repeated actions become your habits. Your habits will shape your character.

Your thought-life is the thread that connects your beliefs to your character and it determines the lifestyle you live—whether you **live to win** or live to lose. When you believe wrong, you will

21

begin to speak wrong (negative) words and your consistently wrong words will eventually lead you to wrong choices and wrong actions. If you're unsure of what's right or wrong in a particular circumstance, look to God's Word to provide the answer. It always leads to "right".

So look to Jesus. He will help you in your thought-life because He wants you to believe right. Then, the thread connecting your thoughts to your words, decisions, and actions will lead to godly and *victorious* habits that shape your character.

Winner's Viewpoint

Your thoughts and words influence how your life turns out.

Victory Prayer Starter

Lord Jesus, Your thoughts are above my thoughts. Please give me wisdom about

_____

_____

Today, I'm grateful for this Win:

Thank you, Lord Jesus, for how You gave me victory in

_____

_____

Day 9

No Condemnation

Victory Verse

Therefore there is now no condemnation [no guilty verdict, no punishment] for those who are in Christ Jesus [who believe in Him as personal Lord and Savior].
Romans 8:1 AMP

Winner's Inspiration

Guilt and self-condemnation frequently get in the way. But Romans 8:1 helps you see that believing that God condemns you is *wrong* believing.

"No condemnation" is your truth because Jesus did the ultimate good thing on your behalf. He died to give you a new position that has no punishment attached to it. It's a position of victory that comes with a clear conscience and a great inheritance. Because of that, you can choose to believe God's words and His promises. Believe that good things are coming your way.

Believing His words will transform your fear into faith and your tragedy into triumph. Let His Word be a tool you use, your personal hammer, to chisel away and break into pieces the

23

stubborn things that bind you in the grip of fear and unbelief (see Jeremiah 23:29).

Winner's Viewpoint

You can change how your life is being played out simply by changing what you believe about yourself.

Victory Prayer Starter

Lord Jesus, thank you that You made it possible for me to no longer feel condemned about

_____

_____

_____

_____

Today, I'm grateful for this Win:

Thank you, Lord Jesus, for how You gave me victory in

_____

_____

_____

_____

Day 10

Believe You're Loved

Victory Verse

For they will see that you love each one of them with the same passionate love that you have for me.
John 17:23 TPT

Winner's Inspiration

What goes into your mind determines what you believe. What you believe determines who you are, what you have, and what you do.

Beliefs evolve when you allow yourself to move past fears and discover freedom and the victories awaiting you on the other side.

Believe that God the Father loves you just like He loves Jesus. That's something that I've only been learning in recent years, because I always thought Jesus was JESUS, so how could God possibly love me like He loves Him? But John 17:23 says otherwise. It reveals that *God the Father loves us just as much as He loves Jesus*. It's imperative that you believe that this tiny but very important piece of God's Word is true in your own life.

Winner's Viewpoint

I stand in the same flow of love from the Father that Jesus does. Acknowledging His love puts me in a position of victory!

Victory Prayer Starter

Lord Jesus, You made it possible for me to enjoy the love of the Father so that I can

_____

_____

_____

_____

Today, I'm grateful for this Win:

Thank you, Lord Jesus, for how You gave me victory in

_____

_____

_____

_____

_____

Day 11

The Seed You Need

Victory Verse

The words I have spoken to you are spirit and life.
John 6:63 AMP

Winner's Inspiration

We must know about *and* believe God's love for us. It's important to trust Him.

Will you believe that God's word is *your* truth? Believe that it is the seed *you* need in order to have a future filled with multiple victories. God's Word contains the power you need for victory, and the way you tap into that power is through hearing and believing what God has said.

Believe that Jesus' work on the cross was perfect. Through His perfectly obedient life, He satisfied every requirement of God. God the Father accepted Jesus' obedience on behalf of all mankind. In our stead, Jesus also took upon Himself *all* of God's wrath that was kindled by *our* disobedience. In one fell

27

swoop, He cleared away all the punishment that we deserved by taking it upon Himself on the cross.

God is not angry with us anymore. Because of Jesus' perfect work, we don't have to endure God's anger. Proof of that is also found in I Thessalonians 5:9 NLT: "For God chose to save us, through our Lord Jesus Christ, not to pour out his anger on us." God's love is intentional. He wants us to receive loving salvation, not angry condemnation.

Winner's Viewpoint

Jesus isn't pointing His finger at me about my wrongs. He simply wants me to trust Him because He came to save me.

Victory Prayer Starter

Lord Jesus, You did not come to condemn us. Help me to remember that when

_____

_____

Today, I'm grateful for this Win:

Thank you, Lord Jesus, for how You gave me victory in

_____

_____

A Roller Coaster Ride

Victory Verse

*For I know the plans I have for you, declares the Lord,
plans to prosper you and not to harm you,
plans to give you hope and a future.*
Jeremiah 29:11 NIV

Winner's Inspiration

You don't have to work hard at believing. Jesus has said that He wants you to experience rest with Him so you can enjoy life's ride! You can find joy in knowing that God has gone ahead of you to prepare the way to your destination. The destination is good and so is His plan for getting you there. You do have a choice in this journey: to worry and be fearful of what could possibly happen or to enjoy getting there by resting in Him.

For example, everybody on a roller coaster is going to the same destination. But at the end, some people were so afraid and tense throughout the entire ride that they could not enjoy it and got off never wanting to try it again. Others, who threw their arms up, smiled, and kept their eyes open because they chose to relax and enjoy the ride, are more likely to get off wanting to try the ride again.

Become carefree by looking to and trusting in Jesus' goodness. Rest, knowing that everything is not on your shoulders because you've given it to Him. Just focus on the thought, "God's got this."

Winner's Viewpoint

God is always with me.

There is no need for me to worry or fear.

Victory Prayer Starter

Lord Jesus, sometimes I feel anxious about

_____

_____

_____

Today, I'm grateful for this Win:

Thank you, Lord Jesus, for how You gave me victory in

_____

_____

_____

Day 13

Jesus As Your Pinch Hitter

Victory Verse

Don't worry about anything; instead, pray about everything.
Tell God what you need, and thank him for all he has done.
Philippians 4:6 NLT

Winner's Inspiration

In baseball, the pinch hitter comes in as a substitute for a player that is injured, tired, or not performing well. They finish the remainder of the game for that player. Maybe you could think of it this way: Jesus became your pinch hitter and took on all the wrath and punishment that you should have endured.

So, if Jesus steps in as your pinch hitter, imagine He would say, "Go stand over there, I've got this. Watch me and rest, trusting that I'm going to do a great job of taking care of things out there in the field of life." Wouldn't you enjoy resting, knowing that He's working on your behalf?

How do you empower yourself to believe these things that Jesus did on our behalf so that you can enjoy life? Again, it boils down to using the right equipment, and that equipment is the Bible. Spend time in God's Word—making sure that as you're reading it you're also *hearing* it. Faith comes as a consequence of repeatedly hearing the promises and words of God.

Winner's Viewpoint

Allowing Jesus to be my substitute

is the best decision I could make!

Victory Prayer Starter

Lord Jesus, help me spend time in Your Word and building my faith so that

_____

_____

_____

_____

Today, I'm grateful for this Win:

Thank you, Lord Jesus, for how You gave me victory in

_____

_____

_____

_____

Day 14

The BEST Life Coach for You

Victory Verse

For no matter how many promises God has made,
they are "Yes" in Christ.
And so through Him the "Amen" is spoken
by us to the glory of God.
2 Corinthians 1:20 NIV

Winner's Inspiration

Much like a life coach who helps a client make positive changes in their life, the Holy Spirit is also coaching us. He's letting us know that we've got to change how we think and what we believe in order to live life purposefully and to the best of our ability. And what are the benefits of doing that?

If you are repeatedly reminding yourself of those positive and purposeful things, they become a part of you, as if you're on autopilot. As a friend once told me, "practice makes permanent!" Repetition empowers your mind to make a shift so that believing—being certain about a God-promised outcome— becomes automatic.

When you renew your mind to the Word of God, along with the practical and helpful insights the Holy Spirit brings, you will live a life of greater victory, power, and favor. This is what becomes your new normal, your new way of believing and living. This new way of believing is based upon having confidence that God has said, "Yes" to *everything* He has promised. His promises are certain. You can confidently count on His fulfillment of them.

Winner's Viewpoint

To succeed within God's plan, you have to consistently keep living by faith. Holy Spirit helps me with that.

Victory Prayer Starter

Lord Jesus, please show me how to confidently count on Your fulfillment of Your promise to

_____

_____

_____

Today, I'm grateful for this Win:

Thank you, Lord Jesus, for how You gave me victory in

_____

_____

Day 15

Renew Your Mind

Victory Verse

Don't copy the behavior and customs of this world, but let God transform you into a new person by changing the way you think. Then you will learn to know God's will for you, which is good and pleasing and perfect.
Romans 12:2 NLT

Winner's Inspiration

What does it mean to renew your mind? It means to change the way you think. But don't change to any random way of thinking. The best renewal of your mind happens when you allow God to work an inner transformation within you and give you a fresh thought life.

It's not about fitting into a mold to be like everyone else. Fitting in to the world's way of doing things isn't God's best for you. His best always involves His Word. Use His Word in your everyday life and embrace all the good that it brings to your mind.

God has promised to love you, no matter what. So fix your attention on Him. Respond to His prompts. He wants to bring out the best in you as you allow your way of thinking to align with His.

Winner's Viewpoint

There's no benefit in living the way the world lives or in imitating its culture. The benefit lies in empowering your mind by reading and hearing God's Word.

Victory Prayer Starter

Lord Jesus, You know my situation. Renew my mind through your Word about

_____

_____

_____

_____

Today, I'm grateful for this Win:

Thank you, Lord Jesus, for how You gave me victory in

_____

_____

_____

_____

Day 16

What Did God Promise?

Victory Verse

God faithfully keeps his promises. He called you to be partners with his Son Jesus Christ our Lord.
1 Corinthians 1:9 GW

Winner's Inspiration

How many times have you believed someone when they made a promise to you and then they did not fulfill it? When a promise is broken, most people decrease the level of trust they have in the person who made the promise.

Remember these Scripture passages that give us assurance that God keeps His promises:

- Not a single one of all the good promises the Lord had given to the family of Israel was left unfulfilled; everything he had spoken came true.
  – Joshua 21:45 NLT

- You know with all your heart and soul that not one of all the good promises the Lord your God gave you has failed. Every promise has been fulfilled; not one has failed. – Joshua 23:14 NIV

Look how good God is at keeping His promises!

Winner's Viewpoint

God does not lie to me. His promises have a 0% failure rate.

Victory Prayer Starter

Lord Jesus, I want to believe that You keep ALL Your promises. When I doubt You, help me to

_____

_____

_____

_____

Today, I'm grateful for this Win:

Thank you, Lord Jesus, for how You gave me victory in

_____

_____

_____

_____

_____

Day 17

You are Blameless

Victory Verse

So now there is no condemnation to those who
belong to Christ Jesus.
Romans 8:1 NLT

Winner's Inspiration

Because of Jesus' sacrifice on the cross, you are now free of condemnation. God sees you through a lens that is covered with the blood of His Son. There's no need to hold on to a guilty conscience. God wants only what's best for you so condemnation has no role in His perspective of you.

He chooses not to pour out anger toward you. Instead, you are blameless in His eyes. That's because He loves you and wants you to live to win! On the day that you received Jesus as Savior, His shed blood was enough to make you righteous (2 Corinthians 5:21). And because you are righteous, you are now eternally blameless. And now that you are seen as blameless, you don't have to hold on to guilt and shame for the wrong things you've done.

Winner's Viewpoint

God loves you. He wants only what's best for you. Therefore, condemnation has no role in His perspective of you.

Victory Prayer Starter

Lord Jesus, You gave Yourself for me and made me righteous in the Father's eyes. Please help me to remember that You don't condemn me for

_____

_____

_____

_____

Today, I'm grateful for this Win:

Thank you, Lord Jesus, for how You gave me victory in

_____

_____

_____

_____

_____

Day 18

One Thing God Doesn't Remember

Victory Verse

And I will be merciful to them in their wrongdoings, and I will remember their sins no more.
Hebrews 8:12 TLB

Winner's Inspiration

Even though God knows everything about you, He found it important to make a promise to forget one thing. That one thing is your sin.

When you made Jesus the Lord of your life, you were able to take God up on this offer to free you from the burden of feeling guilty when you approach Him. Because He has *chosen* to forget the wrong things you've done, you can go to Him without feeling ashamed. Instead, you can approach Him knowing that you are loved.

The promise God made in Hebrews 8:12 to never remember your sins is one you can count on!

Winner's Viewpoint

God sees you through the lens of the cross. Jesus' blood washed you clean of all sins so that there's no need for you to feel ashamed in His presence.

Victory Prayer Starter

Heavenly Father, You said You are merciful when You see my wrongdoing. That makes me feel _____

_____

_____

_____

_____

Today, I'm grateful for this Win:

Thank you, Lord Jesus, for how You gave me victory in

_____

_____

_____

_____

_____

Day 19

Can a Christian Have Limited Faith?

Victory Verse

But blessed are those who haven't seen me and believe anyway.
John 20:29 TLB

Winner's Inspiration

Thomas, one of the disciples of Jesus, became well known as "Doubting Thomas" because of his thought process of needing to see something before he would believe it. The joy that the other disciples were expressing about having seen the resurrected Jesus was not enough to convince Thomas that Jesus was alive. He declared that not only would he have to see Jesus for himself, he'd need to touch Jesus as well.

When Jesus came back to visit again, Thomas was there. He didn't ask Jesus if he could touch Him. But Jesus knew that Thomas had previously said he'd need to experience the physical in order to believe the spiritual. Jesus admonished Thomas, telling him, "Don't be an unbeliever. Be a believer!"

Winner's Viewpoint

Be a believer! Most people think, "I'll believe it when I see it." But God wants us to think, "I'll see it when I believe it."

Victory Prayer Starter

Lord Jesus, help me to believe Your promises so that

_____

_____

_____

_____

Today, I'm grateful for this Win:

Thank you, Lord Jesus, for how You gave me victory in

_____

_____

_____

_____

_____

Day 20

What is Doubt?

Victory Verse

But the Lord God says: This plan will not succeed…
You don't believe me? If you want me to protect you,
you must learn to believe what I say.
Isaiah 7:7, 9 TLB

Winner's Inspiration

Doubt is always a product of deceit and a consequence of distance. Doubt arises due to our being deceived into thinking that God is not on our side in the midst of our trouble. It increases when we have distanced ourselves from the Word; it also minimizes the role and effectiveness of our prayer. It infiltrates our circumstances and reduces our trust because we are distracted from God's promises.

Doubt is our automatic response when we don't look to Jesus in order to keep our focus fixed on His love for us.

Winner's Viewpoint

Doubt and reliance on people, instead of on God, can lead to undesirable consequences. Trust God!

Victory Prayer Starter

Lord Jesus, when I find myself doubting whether Your way is the best way, please _____

_____

_____

_____

_____

Today, I'm grateful for this Win:

Thank you, Lord Jesus, for how You gave me victory in

_____

_____

_____

_____

_____

Day 21

It's Your Choice to Believe

Victory Verse

You can never please God without faith,
without depending on Him.
Hebrews 11:6 TLB

Winner's Inspiration

It is up to you to build your belief in the good things God has planned for you. Because He loves you, He has already provided every good thing to you through his Son, Jesus. It's your choice to believe in His **no-matter-what** kind of love. Believing this love is the foundation of receiving those good things.

Believe that God's desire is for you to live above the things you currently struggle with, even to live without the things you struggle with. Jesus came to give you life more abundantly, life that overflows with favor. He wants you to enjoy his blessings in every area of your life. You can begin to do this by simply being more conscious of Jesus' love for you.

Winner's Viewpoint

God is a Rewarder for those who believe that His Word is the Truth for their personal circumstances.

Victory Prayer Starter

Lord Jesus, I choose to believe in Your **no-matter-what** kind of love._____

_____

_____

_____

Today, I'm grateful for this Win:

Thank you, Lord Jesus, for how You gave me victory in

_____

_____

_____

_____

_____

Day 22

Real Love

Victory Verse

I love you with an everlasting love.
So I will continue to show you my kindness.
Jeremiah 31:3 GW

Winner's Inspiration

Real love—God's love— is continual, long, and drawn out; it's forever moving forward and always giving to others.

God *is* love. Love eagerly pursues us. It longs for us and desires us. It wants more than companionship—it desires and delights in intimacy. Love is vibrant, alive, always germinating, always producing fruit—joy, peace, patience, gentleness, and more (Galatians 5:22,23). Get to know and believe the love God has for *you*.

As you believe His love on a deeper, more personal level— one where you believe His love for *you* is true— you'll find your faith flows more easily.

BELIEVE YOU CAN REIGN IN LIFE!

Winner's Viewpoint

Be more conscious of Jesus' love for *you*.

Victory Prayer Starter

Lord Jesus, I want to know your love more deeply. Please

_____

_____

_____

_____

Today, I'm grateful for this Win:

Thank you, Lord Jesus, for how You gave me victory in

_____

_____

_____

_____

Day 23

Whose Team Are You On?

Victory Verse

Jesus looked at them intently, then said, "Without God, it is utterly impossible. But with God everything is possible."
Mark 10:27 TLB

Winner's Inspiration

In today's Victory Verse, the word "with" is defined as "in close proximity to" (according Strong's Concordance).

So if you read that Scripture again, inserting that definition, it takes on a whole new meaning. It's as if Jesus was saying, "If you are relying on yourself or teaming up with and relying only on others, the thing you desire is impossible. But when you team up with Me and you trust Me, you'll stay in close proximity to Me so that you and I can do this together. Then all things are possible."

Truly, some things are impossible with man. However, **all** things are possible with the Lord!

Winner's Viewpoint

Staying near Jesus helps me to see that all things are possible.

Victory Prayer Starter

Lord Jesus, I want to be on Your team, relying on You to make me a winner. I ask You to please

_____

_____

_____

_____

_____

_____

Today, I'm grateful for this Win:

Thank you, Lord Jesus, for how You gave me victory in

_____

_____

_____

_____

_____

The Definition of Trust

Victory Verse

*Move your heart closer and closer to God,
and he will come even closer to you.*
James 4:8 TPT

Winner's Inspiration

Trust is the result of increasingly drawing near to God through His Word and prayer. It infiltrates our circumstances and erases our doubt when we focus on and verbally affirm His promises. Trust is our automatic response when we have practiced looking to Jesus in the Word and acknowledging His love for us.

Jesus challenged Martha to trust Him in the midst of a seemingly hopeless situation—the death of her brother Lazarus (John 11:40). He said, "If you would believe, you would see." This is totally contrary to what most folks think today. They are determined not to believe until they see! But, Martha believed and waited expectantly to see the works of God and she was not disappointed. Lazarus was raised from the dead. Martha's belief came before Martha's seeing.

Martha made a decision to trust Jesus' instruction to believe that He would change her circumstances even though she didn't yet see a change. His words compelled her to trust that she would see something good happen if she would believe In His love, power, and willingness.

Winner's Viewpoint

Doubt is a consequence of distance from the Lord. Conversely, trust is the consequence of closeness to the Lord.

Victory Prayer Starter

Lord Jesus, show me how to trust You more. I need to trust you about_____

_____

_____

_____

Today, I'm grateful for this Win:

Thank you, Lord Jesus, for how You gave me victory in

_____

_____

_____

Day 25

It's Never Useless to Include Jesus

Victory Verse

*Ignoring what they said, Jesus told the synagogue ruler
[Jairus],"Don't be afraid; just believe."*
Mark 5:36 NIV

Winner's Inspiration

Most people think, "I'll believe it when I see it." God wants us to think, "I'll see it because I believe it!"

Jesus helped us understand that point. Jairus sought out Jesus to come to his home and heal his daughter. His daughter was on the verge of dying (Luke 8:41). As they walked to Jairus' home, Jesus made a stop to heal a woman that had endured a medical issue for many years. That must have caused much anxiety for Jairus.

When they finally were on their way again, a servant came and told Jairus it was useless to bring Jesus because his daughter had died. But upon hearing this news, Jesus encouraged Jairus, to "fear not, only believe."

This anxious father was obedient to Jesus' directive. Here's where we see that it's **never** useless to bring Jesus into our circumstances! *After believing* that Jesus would handle his problem, Jairus *saw* the miraculous result—Jesus brought his daughter back to life *and* made her completely well.

Winner's Viewpoint

In God's system, it's *never* useless to get Jesus involved!

Victory Prayer Starter

Lord Jesus, help me to believe that your promises are true for *me*.

Please_____

_____

_____

_____

Today, I'm grateful for this Win:

Thank you, Lord Jesus, for how You gave me victory in

_____

_____

_____

Day 26

When Your Belief is Senses-Based

Victory Verse

Blessed are those who have not seen and yet have believed.
John 20:29 NIV

Winner's Inspiration

Have you ever based your belief only on what you've seen or otherwise experienced through your natural senses? Of course, we all have! It's best to minimize that way of thinking. But one of Jesus' disciples, "Doubting Thomas," is known for declaring how his belief would only be based on what he could see or touch.

His belief was based on what *he* could do, and what *he* could experience in the natural realm with his senses. It was a lost opportunity to have, show, and exercise his faith. Jesus appeared and challenged Thomas to not be faithless and unbelieving but instead to continually believe. Jesus knew that without faith, Thomas would be limited to the very narrow world of the natural realm, comprehended only by his senses.

By doing so, he would not experience the supernatural blessings that belief in Jesus' resurrection could bring.

Winner's Viewpoint

Decide to believe and to stop doubting.

Victory Prayer Starter

Lord Jesus, help me to believe in what You say, not what I sense.

Please_____

_____

_____

_____

Today, I'm grateful for this Win:

Thank you, Lord Jesus, for how You gave me victory in

_____

_____

_____

_____

_____

Day 27

The Fear Factor

Victory Verse

There is no fear in love.
1John 4:18

Winner's Inspiration

A re *you* afraid to believe? Faith is how we make contact with God. It keeps us aware of His love, power, and favor.

Faith involves seeing the invisible with the mind.

> *"Faith led Moses to leave Egypt and he was not*
> *afraid of the king's anger.*
> *Moses didn't give up but **continued as if he could***
> ***actually see the invisible God."***
> Hebrews 11:27 GW (emphasis mine)

Faith requires the mind to look to Jesus with perseverance. If the mind is cluttered with negative thoughts, it is distracted from looking to Jesus and therefore, faith gets diminished. It's important to keep your focus on Jesus' love for you so that you're not fearful in doing what you were born to accomplish!

Winner's Viewpoint

Faith is how we make contact with God and live without fear.

Victory Prayer Starter

Lord Jesus, my faith is in You and all that You accomplished on the cross on my behalf even before I was born. Please

_____

_____

_____

_____

Today, I'm grateful for this Win:

Thank you, Lord Jesus, for how You gave me victory in

_____

_____

_____

_____

_____

Day 28

Stand Firm in Your Faith

Victory Verse

Remember to stay alert and hold firmly to all that you believe.
Be mighty and full of courage.
1 Corinthians 16:13 TPT

Winner's Inspiration

Right in the middle of giving his travel plans and some final instructions to those in the church at Corinth, Paul makes a seemingly out-of-place statement in today's Victory Verse. He was encouraging them (and us) to hold firmly to all that they *believe*.

The Message Bible puts it this way:

Keep your eyes open, hold tight to your convictions, give it all
you've got, be resolute, and love without stopping.

But what did Paul want the people to believe and hold tightly to? Their belief in Jesus and His very personal love for each person. Paul knew that if the people trusted in God's love for them they could proceed to expand their church resolutely and courageously.

The same is true for us today. When we trust in God's love, when we know that we can say, "God loves *me*," we can proceed to live our lives as victors. This is because we are sure that God's got our back as we stand firm in our faith in Him.

Winner's Viewpoint

In the midst of whatever I'm facing, I choose to hold firmly to my faith in God's love for me.

Victory Prayer Starter

Lord Jesus, show me how to keep a tight grip on my faith for

_____

_____

_____

_____

Today, I'm grateful for this Win:

Thank you, Lord Jesus, for how You gave me victory in

_____

_____

_____

Day 29

Maybe Deflated But Never Defeated

Victory Verse

Looking unto Jesus, the Author and Finisher of our faith.
Hebrews 12:2

Winner's Inspiration

Have you ever had the wind knocked out of you? It's the result of a hard blow to your mid-section which temporarily sends your diaphragm into spasms. You probably felt like you couldn't catch your breath and that you needed to stop what you were doing. What happened inside your body is that your lungs became deflated as your diaphragm stayed contracted. But, after a minute or so, the diaphragm resumes its normal function and you're able to take a deep breath and resume your activity.

Sometimes life can feel that way— like you can't take the next step because something has made you feel emotionally or spiritually deflated. But the good thing is, if you've made Jesus your Savior, *and you invite Him into your circumstances*, He will help you recover your sense of victory. Then you're able to move forward.

Because you're in Him, you get to take part in His victory. You're on Jesus' team, so you have the right to enjoy His victory over *everything* that makes you feel defeated. You have the right to live to win!

Winner's Viewpoint

Even if Jesus does all the heavy lifting, I'm still a victor because He gave me the right to be a partaker of *His* victory!

Victory Prayer Starter

Lord Jesus, help me to look to You and see how You've empowered me to live like a victor so that

_____

_____

_____

_____

Today, I'm grateful for this Win:

Thank you, Lord Jesus, for how You gave me victory in

_____

_____

_____

Day 30

Believe in God's Wisdom

Victory Verse

For God intended that your faith not be established on man's wisdom but by trusting in His almighty power.
1 Corinthians 2:5 TPT

Winner's Inspiration

What would you say is the foundation of your faith? Is it your ability to do something good for others? Or is it based on what your parents' faith looked like?

God's grace is available 24/7 to give us the wisdom we need for whatever we face. It makes the Father happy when we ask for His wisdom about our circumstance. He is always willing to give it to us (James 1:5). This helps our soul to rest when we know that we're depending on His wisdom and not our own.

God's wisdom helps us to be active in the realm of authority that we have in Christ. We can maintain peace in our lives when we live believing and using His wisdom.

Winner's Viewpoint

To fully depend on the wisdom of God gives us power!

Victory Prayer Starter

Lord Jesus, God's Word says that if I ask You for wisdom, you will give it to me abundantly. I need Your wisdom about

_____

_____

_____

_____

Today, I'm grateful for this Win:

Thank you, Lord Jesus, for how You gave me victory in

_____

_____

_____

_____

_____

Day 31

You're Authorized to Reign in Life

Victory Verse

For if, by the trespass of the one man, death reigned through that one man, how much more will those who receive God's abundant provision of grace and of the gift of righteousness reign in life through the one man, Jesus Christ!
Romans 5:17 NIV

Winner's Inspiration

J esus has put you in the seat of authority because He wants you to reign in life. He gave His life for that very reason— so that *you* can live out your days with the knowledge that you have been authorized to rule over your circumstances.

Here are a few ways to rule from that seat of authority He has given you:

• Feed on God's Word — hear it, read it, meditate on it (Matthew 4:4; Psalm 119:15).

• Believe in His Word that says you have power over the enemy (Mark 16:17-20).

- Be humble. Acknowledge that the power you exercise comes from God (James 4:10).

- Have a sense of boldness and courage (Hebrews 13:6).

- Use the name of Jesus and bring God on the scene (Acts 3:6).

Winner's Viewpoint

I am seated with Christ in a position of *rest and authority*.

Victory Prayer Starter

Lord Jesus, show me how to actively use Your authority in this situation of

_____

_____

_____

_____

Today, I'm grateful for this Win:

Thank you, Lord Jesus, for how You gave me victory in

_____

_____

_____

_____

_____

SALVATION PRAYER

If you've never asked Jesus to come into your life, now is a good time to do so. Pray this prayer out loud:

Dear God, I admit that I am not right with You. I ask You to forgive me of all my sins. I invite Jesus to rule and reign in my life from this day forward. I believe with my heart that Jesus is Lord and You raised Him from the dead. I confess with my mouth that He is now my Savior.

Thank You for saving me!

Please make me the person You want me to be.

I pray this in Jesus' name, Amen.

*****

If you prayed this prayer, heaven is rejoicing! Jesus has come into your life and His Holy Spirit now lives in you *forever*. You have become a child of God, positioned for VICTORY because of His love for you.

Where Do I Go From Here?

Now that you've completed 31 days of focusing on what you believe, I hope you feel stronger in your spirit and that you firmly believe you were created to reign in life!

What are some of the obstacles you uncovered that were keeping you from fully believing it's God's intention for you to reign in your everyday life?

You might be wondering what to do about this. I have a coaching program that can help you to continue to make progress in overcoming obstacles and more firmly establishing a victorious lifestyle.

I'm happy to provide you with a complimentary discovery session with me so that we can see if **iHope Coaching** will be a good fit in helping you determine *and* execute some good next steps toward victorious living. To take me up on this completely free offer, schedule the session at www.calendly.com/hopecoach.

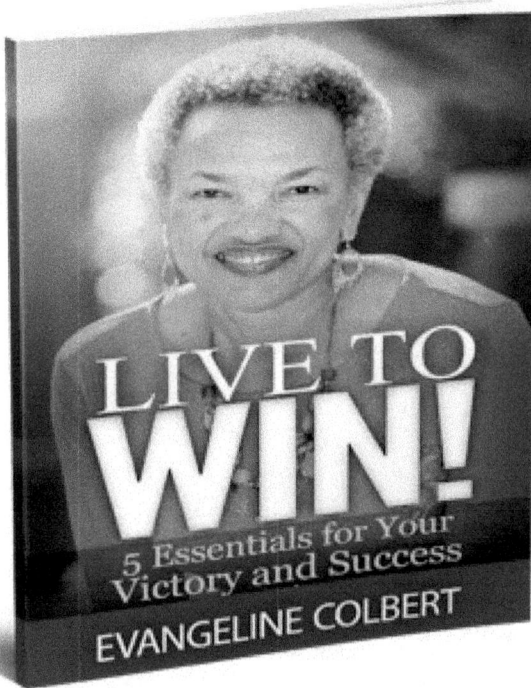

The daily readings you just completed were taken from Evangeline's book, *Live to Win*.

You can find encouragement on all 5 essentials for your victory and success as you read *Live to Wi*n, available from Amazon and other booksellers.

Find all of Evangeline's books at BooksByEvangeline.com

BELIEVE YOU CAN REIGN IN LIFE!

www.ingramcontent.com/pod-product-compliance
Lightning Source LLC
Chambersburg PA
CBHW071930020426
42331CB00010B/2796